# College Planning
# Quick Guide
## Texas Edition

MYCHAL WYNN

Wynn, Mychal.
  College planning quick guide / Mychal Wynn. -- Texas ed.

    p. ; cm.

  "The material contained in this book has been taken from the book 'A High School Plan for Students
with College-Bound Dreams' and contains information specific to Texas secondary schools and the
Texas university system."--T.p. verso.
  Includes index.
  ISBN-13: 978-1-880463-58-1
  ISBN-10: 1-880463-58-X

  1. Academic achievement--Texas.  2. High school students--Texas--Life skills guides.  3. College
applications--Texas--Handbooks, manuals, etc.  4. College choice--Handbooks, manuals, etc.  5.
Universities and colleges--Texas--Admission--Handbooks, manuals, etc.  I. Title.  II. Title: High school
plan for students with college-bound dreams.

LB2350 .W961 2013
373.18/09764                                                                                    2012913574

*Rising Sun Publishing, Inc.*
*P.O. Box 70906*
*Marietta, GA 30007-0906*
*770.518.0369/800.524.2813*
*FAX 770.587.0862*
*E-mail: info@rspublishing.com*
*Web site: www.rspublishing.com*

Printed in the United States of America.

# Acknowledgments

I would like to acknowledge former Texas A&M International University GEAR UP IV Coordinator, Mashyell Calderon, for suggesting the *Texas Edition*. Her passion for guiding parents and students and widening the primary-to-postsecondary pathway to college are reflected in the specific strategies provided for Texas resident students. I would also like to acknowledge the contribution of Patsy Caudill and Linda Currier for their critical review and invaluable suggestions to ensure the specific information and strategies offered for resident students interested in entering the Texas university system are practical and doable for parents and students.

# Table of Contents

# Introduction to the Texas Edition

While states implement the *Common Core State Standards* to increase the number of students prepared to pursue college and careers, college admissions is the most competitive ever, student loan debt is the highest ever, and the process of preparing students for college from elementary school through high school is perhaps, the most complicated ever. According to the 2012 ACT exam results [www.act.org], over 8 out of 10 students want to obtain a 4-year college degree or higher, however, less than half of all students are ready for college after graduating from high school.

The information provided will not only expand parent and student understanding of the college admissions process, it is intended to stimulate conversations about the types of jobs and careers students may aspire to pursue, level of income they wish to earn, and the education that will be required. This book is also intended to guide conversations between parents and students, and the teachers, counselors, and community and faith-based organizations willing to assist students in developing their college-bound plans or navigating the college admissions process.

Parents and students will find comprehensive, yet easy to read, information outlining the Texas high school graduation requirements and some of the many resources available to Texas resident-students to support their college-bound dreams and aspirations. Successful college planning involves developing a comprehensive elementary school-through-high school plan of coursework and activities, researching colleges, visiting college campuses, identifying scholarships and other sources of financial aid, and most of all, beginning the conversation about college years before a student enters high school.

In addition to the 14 chapters and 70 strategies offered, the *Texas Supplement* at the end of the book will guide students to the websites of some of the 104 public and 44 independent institutions in the Texas university and community college system. Whether a student plans to begin in the Texas Community College system or enter directly into a 4-year college or university, the information will assist each student in developing the college-bound plan most reflective of his or her personal situation, college preparation, and financial need.

# From the Author

I am a first generation college student, having graduated with honors from Boston's Northeastern University, the only college to which I applied. My wife and I have two sons who are currently attending college. Our older son is a senior at Amherst College and our younger son is the recipient of the Gates Millennium Scholarship and a freshman at Morehouse College. They have different gifts and talents and different educational and career aspirations. To ensure that our sons had the best college and scholarship opportunities, and long before either of them had considered where they would attend college, my wife and I read books, engaged in research, visited schools, and worked with teachers and counselors in each of their elementary, middle, and high schools. We spent thousands of hours reading, researching, and developing strategies.

This book, the middle school and high school books in the college planning series, and my college planning blog (*www.accessandequity.org/blog*) shares what we have learned and provides insight, strategies, research, and the most currently available information to assist all students in pursuing their educational and career aspirations.

**Parents must talk to their children about college!**

The Texas Comprehensive Center Briefing Paper on *Parent and Community Involvement in a College/Career-Ready Culture* notes:

*Some of the key findings of available research indicate that students with involved parents, no matter what their income or background, are more likely to:*

- *Earn high grades and test scores and enroll in higher-level programs*

- *Pass their classes, earn credits, and be promoted*

- *Attend school regularly*

- *Graduate and go on to postsecondary education*

The most consistent finding in studies of parental involvement was "the importance of parents' educational aspirations for their children."

# Overview

The three primary areas of focus for a college-bound student are:

1. Meeting your high school graduation requirements.
2. Becoming a strong candidate for admissions to your first-choice colleges and being prepared to succeed academically once you get there.
3. Meeting your EFC (Expected Family Contribution) for college tuition, room, and board.

There will be two additional areas of focus for the recruited college-bound athlete:

4. Registering with the NCAA Clearinghouse and meeting the NCAA qualifications for a student-athlete.
5. Developing an athletic profile/portfolio specific to your sport or a video showcasing your unique athletic skills and abilities.

# 1: develop a four-fold strategy

There are four broad categories that will ultimately determine how successful you are in developing your college-bound plan.

## Academics

- Meeting high school graduation requirements
- Meeting college admission standards
- Coursework
- Grades
- Class rank
- High School Profile
- STARR, SAT, SAT Subject Tests, PSAT, ACT, and AP exam scores
- Awards, honors, noteworthy academic achievements and recognition

## Extracurricular Activities

- Sports
- Clubs
- Special programs
- Student organizations
- Community service
- Volunteer hours
- Work experience

## Personal Qualities

- Essay
- Interview
- Recommendations
- Contribution to your school community
- Unique talent (e.g., artistic, musical, athletic, dance, mathematical, or public speaking)
- Personal achievements (e.g., overcoming adversity, resiliency, integrity, worthy ideals, or innovation)

# Intangible and Other Influencing Factors

- Ethnicity

- Gender

- Socioeconomic background

- Geographical area

- Involvement in a club or activity for which the college has a unique need, e.g., genius-level I.Q., classical pianist, point guard, martial arts instructor, swimmer, or 400-meter sprinter

---

## 2: identify your dreams

---

What are your dreams and aspirations—the places you want to go, things you want to experience, changes you want to make in your home, community, or in the world itself? Where do you find your joy? What type of people do you prefer being around? What type of job would you do even if you did not get paid to do it? Or, better yet, what is your purpose? Are you passionate about music, art, science, math, sports, or social issues? Do you prefer working with people or in isolation? Do you have a passion to be an entertainer or to pursue public service? Do you have a passion to become a teacher or to build a business? Would you prefer to write a book, give a lecture, or both? Answering such questions will help you to identify the classes that will expand your knowledge, nurture your passions, and best prepare you for the college experience you are interested in pursuing.

## 3: identify your dream schools

1. Make a list of things you most enjoy doing, e.g., traveling, shopping, sports, surfing, roller skating, music, dressing up, dressing down, cooking, eating, telling jokes, talking on the phone, socializing, dancing, singing, playing a musical instrument, solving puzzles, writing poetry, drawing cartoons, playing computer games, lifting weights, studying martial arts, running marathons, playing chess, building model airplanes, camping, fishing, golfing, rock climbing, etc.

2. Make a list of the type of people and places you enjoy, e.g., large crowds, small groups, debating/discussing political and social issues, attending concerts or sporting events, exercising, theatrical performances, starting businesses, running a political campaign, pursuing a spiritual journey, attending social functions, exploring and discovering, creating and developing, living in a mansion, or living on a farm.

3. Make a list of the types of careers that will allow you to do those things on your first list and work with the type of people or live in the places on your second list.

Whether you have dreamed of becoming a Longhorn® or Aggie®, entering one of the U.S. Military Service Academies, or being admitted into one of the country's most highly selective colleges and universities like Amherst, Williams, Harvard, Yale, MIT, Caltech, Stanford, or Duke—choose a college that will allow you to pursue your passions, surround you with the type of people you enjoy, and nurture your intellectual development, creative capacity, and social consciousness. In essence, carefully choose a place to live, grow, and enjoy life for the four years following high school.

# 4: know what makes you special

After successfully progressing through elementary and middle school, the question for you to ask yourself as you enter high school is, "When I graduate from high school, why would a college want to admit me into its freshman class? What will be special about me and what will I be able to contribute to its school community?"

Asking that question as you enter high school will help you to better understand how to take advantage of the many programs and opportunities available at your high school and accessible to aspiring college students over the course of your four-year high school experience. Whether you are passionate about athletics, politics, dance, music, science, mathematics, journalism, poetry, art, philosophy, social issues, technology, or speech and debate, your high school years will have a significant impact on the scope and depth of the college application packages you prepare as a high school junior and senior. Entering high school with the passionate desire to pursue something, become something, discover something, change something, or fulfill some purpose will guide your intellectual, spiritual, moral, physical, and creative development in ways, that, will enable you to sit in a college interview and say, "I have had a passion to do ... since I entered high school; this is what I have done and why I want to continue my studies at your college."

Your school performance—academic achievement, coursework, extracurricular activities, community service, volunteer hours, standardized test scores, hobbies, interests, leadership, and personal achievements—together with your values, beliefs, race, gender, culture, family background, and life experiences provide a testimony to your uniqueness and evidence of the special contribution you could make to a college community.

# 5: build relationships

Developing and executing an effective college-bound plan will require that you build relationships with several groups of people. Colleges will evaluate your application in part based on recommendations from your high school teachers and counselor; your meaningful involvement in clubs, organizations, school and community service projects; and your involvement in sports, band, cheerleading, or other special-interest activities. The relationships you develop with tutors and study groups will also greatly contribute to your academic success. Consider the following people as excellent sources for letters of recommendation:

- Counselor
- Coaches
- Faculty Advisors
- Clergy
- Law Enforcement

- Teachers
- Volunteer Coordinators
- Administrators
- Local Politicians
- An Alumnus

# 6: get organized

Preparing a comprehensive college-bound plan will require that you establish a place to store all of the information you gather over the course of the coming days, weeks, months, or years.

- Set up a *College Planning Notebook* (3-ring binder)
- Set up four file folders or boxes and label them:
    - Academics
    - Programs & Camps
    - Scholarships
    - Awards, Competitions, Internships, & Volunteer Hours
- Set up two boxes and label them:
    - College Information
    - Financial-Aid Information

# 7: identify your team

If you are planning on going to college then you need to affirm that you are going to college. This means that you should be talking about college to your family, friends, teachers, counselors, coaches, mentors, and tutors. The more you talk about college, the more information people will share with you. The more they will confirm or challenge what you think about college, what you are thinking about doing with your life, and whether or not what you are doing now is consistent with where you say you are planning to go.

Your high school counselor (or in some cases a mentor or private counselor) is going to be one of the most important people with whom to share your college dreams. Along with this book, he or she should become an invaluable source of information. It will be your counselor's job to provide you with, or direct you to, the information you need to fulfill your college aspirations. Your counselor may be able to make your work a lot easier by identifying where to get the information you need, assisting in completing the necessary financial-aid forms, and ensuring you fulfill your high school graduation requirements. Eventually, you will have to turn your college application packages in to your counselor, who will have to enclose your high school transcript prior to mailing your materials to the colleges to which you apply.

Working with programs such as GEAR UP, AVID, and Upward Bound, friends, booster clubs, mentoring programs, community and faith-based organizations, and other families will allow you to accomplish much more than by working alone. It will also help you to develop important team-building and leadership skills as you participate in such activities as:

- College Visits
- College Fairs
- Pre-college and Summer Programs
- Internships

- Competitions and Leadership Programs
- Working with Tutors
- SAT, SAT Subject Tests, PSAT, and ACT Prep Programs
- Putting together College Application Packages
- Writing College and Scholarship Essays

# 8: follow your stats

As you enter elementary school, imagine beginning an NBA or WNBA career. Every pass, steal, free throw, three-pointer, blocked shot, and playoff game—every statistic is going to become part of your permanent NBA/WNBA stat sheet. Your elementary and middle school stat sheet—grades, test scores, discipline infractions—will influence your high school opportunities. Your high school stat sheet—awards, grades, test scores, class rank, coursework, extracurricular activities, volunteer hours, community service, creative or artistic achievements—will influence your college and scholarship opportunities.

# Chapter 1

## *Academics*

There is a reason the first area of focus in your high school plan is academics and not because it is first in alphabetical order. Your high school transcript is the most important part of your application package. Whether you are a star athlete, president of the student council, brilliant musician, or the most popular student in your high school, college success ultimately comes down to your ability to successfully complete the coursework.

Athletics, leadership positions, creative or artistic talent, awards and community service may all influence the final decision of a college admissions committee; however, once you are accepted, you will have to complete the coursework to receive your college degree. In the final analysis, your academic ability is still the most important aspect of college preparation.

Your academic performance will include:

- Meeting the Texas Education Agency's high school graduation requirements
- Meeting college admissions standards
- Coursework, grades, class rank, and high school profile
- STARR EOCs, SAT, SAT Subject Tests, ACT, AP, or IB exam scores
- Awards, honors, noteworthy academic achievements and recognition

## 9: maintain a college focus

Although you SHOULD begin middle school with a college focus, you MUST begin high school with a college focus. Whether you are considering going into the military, pursuing a trade, or simply getting a job after high school, you must begin high school with a college focus. Doing so will ensure that you do as much as possible to prepare yourself for college should you decide to attend college after graduating from high school. While the primary focus of this book is on college admissions, keep in mind that there are many postsecondary educational and career opportunities that may lead to something other than a four-year university. A student's passion for cooking may lead to a culinary school, a passion for computer programming may lead to a computer programming or technical school, a passion for a trade may lead to an internship or trade school.

## 10: research colleges

As soon as you begin to develop an idea of the types of colleges in which you are interested, or colleges that offer fields of study in your areas of interest, begin making contact. Colleges keep track of whom, and how often, prospective students contact them. It is never too early in the process to let potential colleges and universities know you have an interest in their programs. Write, call, or e-mail the office of admissions, professors, coaches, departments, or programs to request information. Once you are in their database, they will begin mailing or e-mailing you information on a regular basis. As you begin receiving information, give extra or unwanted information to your counselor so he or she may share the information with other students in the guidance office or counseling center.

## 11: develop a top-ten list

Attempt to identify at least ten colleges in Texas or other parts of the country where you can envision yourself learning, growing, and developing lasting relationships with classmates and professors becoming one of the school's distinguished alumnus. A place where the quality of education will provide you with a degree that will prepare you for a career or graduate school. Place your list in the front of your *College Planning Notebook*, on a wall, or onto your refrigerator— someplace where you will be continually reminded of your high school focus until you can begin checking off those schools where you have been offered admission and the necessary financial aid.

# Chapter 2

## *High School Graduation Requirements*

It is important for you to understand the current Texas Education Agency's high school graduation requirements and track your progress throughout high school. The TEA's website provides the most up to date information:

### *www.tea.state.tx.us/graduation.aspx*

Currently the *Minimum High School Program* requires 22 credits, the *Recommended High School Program* requires 26 credits, and the *Distinguished High School Program* requires 26 credits. Each program has specific course requirements, however, your high school may have various levels and types of courses to meet those requirements. The classes you take and grades you earn will have a profound impact on your application to the Texas university system or to colleges and universities outside of Texas.

For example, Texas A&M notes on their website:

*"Students who graduate from a Texas high school under the recommended or advanced/distinguished high school curriculum will meet Texas A&M's minimum course requirements."*

However, they also note:

*"It is recommended that applicants complete the most challenging and rigourous educational plan available to them during their high school career."*

Students can use the *College Results Online* website to further research how competitive it is to be accepted to Texas A&M:

- 33 percent of students who apply to Texas A&M are denied admission

- The median SAT scores for admitted students are 575 Verbal and 615 Math

- The median ACT Composite score of admitted students is 27

Your high school grades and course schedule must meet the expectations of the colleges you plan to apply to.

# 12: identify STARR requirements

The State of Texas Assessments of Academic Readiness (STAAR™) measures the Texas Essential Knowledge and Skills (TEKS) curriculum standards. There are assessments for students in grades 3 – 8 in the areas of reading, mathematics, writing, science, and social studies; Spanish assessments in grades 3 – 5; and 12 end-of-course (EOC) assessments for high school students in: Algebra I, geometry, Algebra II, biology, chemistry, physics, English I, English II, English III, world geography, world history, and U.S. history.

The Texas Education Agency's website provides complete information, including sample questions (*www.tea.state.tx.us/student.assessment/staar/*). Meet with your counselor to ensure that you are fulfilling the TEA's graduation requirements and that you are enrolled in the necessary classes to prepare for the required grade level assessments or end-of-course exams.

# 13: if you are an athlete

If you are planning on participating in college athletics during your freshman year in college, you must register with the NCAA Clearinghouse (www.ncaaclearinghouse.net). Many athletes register during the summer between their junior and senior year after receiving their junior-year high school transcript. The Clearinghouse outlines the full range of classes, grades, test scores, and recruiting guidelines.

Carefully review the *NCAA Guide for the College-Bound Student-Athlete* (ncaa.org) so you fully understand recruiting guidelines, eligibility requirements, and registration dates. It is possible to fulfill the graduation requirements for your high school and not meet the NCAA eligibility requirements, which would mean that you would not be able to receive a scholarship or be eligible to compete as a college student-athlete.

# Chapter 3

## *Coursework*

You and your parents must take an active role in planning your middle school-through-high school classes. Class requirements vary by high school and can range from unrestricted open enrollment to highly restricted–highly selective student enrollment that requires pre-requisite middle school classes or counselor and teacher approval.

During your final year of middle school or junior high school, your counselor will submit a suggested class schedule to the high school that you will be attending. Nearing the end of the school year or during the summer before entering high school, you will receive your high school class schedule. Carefully review your class schedule to ensure that you will begin on track toward taking the classes that you would like to take during each year of high school.

# 14: take a challenging schedule

When planning your middle school and high school course schedules, begin with the end in mind—consider the type of colleges you will be applying to. Will you want to be ranked in the top ten percent of your high school graduating class so you have automatic admission into the Texas public university system? Will you be applying to a highly-selective college or university like Rice, Brown, NYU, the Naval Academy, Northwestern, or Penn? Wherever you are considering applying to college, visit the college's or university's website and research the type and level of classes they are expecting their incoming freshmen to have taken in high school.

If you are academically prepared and willing to accept the challenge of enrolling in academically rigorous classes such as honors, Pre-AP, AP (Advanced Placement), IB (International Baccalaureate), or dual enrollment, then do so. The sooner you enroll in higher-level classes, the more higher-level classes you will have the opportunity to take throughout high school.

Students who choose to fill their schedules with easy classes and electives severely limit their college choices. Admissions committees at the nation's top colleges will be looking for a challenging academic schedule and examples—either in your coursework or in your teacher recommendations—of your participation in classroom discussions, debates, and active involvement in furthering ideas and opinions.

*When making admission decisions, we look positively upon students who show their commitment to academics by taking the most rigorous coursework available to them. Level of coursework taken is considered in context with the availability of coursework in your high school. (UT Austin website)*

Some colleges will even expect applicants to have engaged in research, published a scientific paper, written original musical compositions, or to have choreographed dance performances.

# 15: know your high school

Admissions committees pay attention to the classes offered at your high school and those that you chose to take. Many of the colleges you apply to will request from your school's counselor, a "School Profile," which outlines the types of classes offered, total number of available honors and AP classes, your high school's state ranking, average SAT scores, etc. The college admissions committee will raise the question, "Did this student take the most challenging classes offered at his or her high school?"

# 16: honors classes

Admissions committees will typically assess a higher value to honors classes. Depending on the subject or teacher, the class may move at a faster pace, involve more work, or require more effort on the part of the student. As a result of the increased difficulty, many school districts provide additional points that are credited to the student's overall GPA resulting in a higher weighted GPA. Talk to your counselor about the "weight" of such classes, as well as the weight of Pre-AP, AP, IB, and dual or joint enrollment classes.

Although a weighted GPA may increase your class ranking, some colleges and scholarship programs (like the Gates Millennium Scholarship) will only consider your unweighted grades, i.e., 'A', 'B', 'C', etc., before receiving the additional points or "weight."

## 17: AP classes

The Advanced Placement program and what are more commonly referred to as 'AP' classes is administered by the College Board (*www.collegeboard.org*). Some school districts also offer Pre-AP classes as preparation for AP classes, which are college-level courses, offered as regular high school classes, and provide students with the opportunity to receive advanced placement or college credit (based on their AP exam scores). AP classes typically represent the most difficult and demanding high school classes and are designed to prepare students for AP exit exams, which are administered once a year in May and usually take two to three hours to complete.

# 18: dual or joint enrollment

Dual or Joint Enrollment programs provide opportunities to enroll in college while completing high school and typically provide students with the opportunity to earn both high school and college credit for successfully completing classes. Some of the benefits of dual or joint enrollment are:

- Classes qualify for college credit, with some also qualifying for high school credit, thereby allowing students to take college classes in place of certain high school classes.

- Classes are usually paid for by the state, college, or local school district.

- Classes provide students with an opportunity to experience college-level classes while still in high school, thereby helping students to know what to expect when they enroll in college full-time.

- Classes enhance a student's college application by indicating that the student is capable of college-level work and may provide early admissions preference at the dual or joint enrollment college.
- Classes provide an opportunity for students to learn from college professors.

---

# 19: take your grades seriously

---

If you have the academic ability to be an 'A' student, then be an 'A' student. If you have friends who do not take academic achievement seriously, do not allow them to keep you from performing at the level of your academic potential. Put yourself in the best possible position to qualify first, for admission, and secondly, for financial aid (i.e., scholarships). Your high school GPA, together with your SAT or ACT scores may significantly increase your chances for college admission and automatically qualify you for a broad range of merit or academic scholarships.

# 20: class rank

Class rank is one of those very important, oftentimes little discussed, statistics you need to be aware. Some colleges have special admissions criteria based on class rank (e.g., top 5 percent, top 10 percent, etc.) and award full scholarships to students who were their high school's Valedictorian or Salutatorian. Current Texas law, guarantees resident-students, who rank in the top ten percent of their high school's graduating class, admission into the Texas public university system. Currently, the only public university in Texas with an exception to the law is UT Austin, which currently admits a maximum of 75 percent of its incoming freshman class under the Top 10 Percent law. This could limit accepted students to those ranked in the top 8 percent of their graduating class. However, class ranking is only one component of your college-bound plan. If you are not ranked in the top ten percent of your high school's graduating class there will still be many college and scholarship opportunities available to you.

# Chapter 4

## *Academic Support*

As you progress through school, you must openly and honestly assess your strengths and weaknesses. Do you have difficulty with math? Is science one of your weakest areas? Do you have difficulty reading or understanding what you have read? Do you have difficulty speaking or writing in a foreign language? Do not allow yourself to get off to a slow start and do not shrug off your weaknesses, "I am just not good at math." You must identify what and whom you need to ensure your academic success. Do not make the mistake of ignoring your weaknesses until you begin failing academically. Elementary school struggles in math will only lead to greater difficulty in middle school and high school math.

# 21: join a study group

Since you are likely to join a study group in college, it would be a good idea to form study groups as early as elementary school. You may find them particularly beneficial in your more challenging subjects—those subjects where you are experiencing difficulty or have an acknowledged weakness.

# 22: get a tutor

Do not get left behind. In subjects like math and science, you may find yourself experiencing difficulty fully understanding scientific concepts or math equations. This does not necessarily have anything to do with your intelligence or the teacher's effectiveness. However, it is your grades that admissions officers are going to be reviewing so it is your responsibility to let the teacher know when you are having difficulty. If you continue to find yourself struggling, it is your responsibility to find a tutor, identify supplemental materials, or an online website like Khan Academy (*www.khanacademy.org/*) where you can view videos and tutorials in math, science, and other subjects. A tutor will have more time to explain problems and concepts in greater detail than what the teacher covers in class and online tutorials will allow you to work problems and reinforce what you are learning in class.

## 23: join an academic club

Consider joining clubs related to your academic areas—science, math, computer programming, foreign language, etc. Students involved in these clubs have probably taken classes that you are going to take and will have comments and information about teachers, tutors, course content, and how to succeed. Some academic clubs receive special recognition at graduation and provide scholarship opportunities.

# Chapter 5

## *Academic Honors*

Begin each school year with a focus on the types of honors, awards, and recognition you would like to receive. Does your elementary school have an honor roll, does your middle have academic awards, does your high school recognize student achievement with awards, cords, pins, trophies, or scholarships? Many of the awards you earn in high school will not only reflect the academic growth from your work in elementary school and middle school, they will be listed on your résumé, and on college and scholarship applications. Keep in mind that no award or recognition is too small to be overlooked.

There are many opportunities for students to be recognized by their school, local community, local government, religious, civic, and professional organizations. To ensure that you do not miss anything when it is time to complete your college application, establish a routine of making note of your awards in your *College Planning Notebook*. Place copies of your report cards, transcripts, test scores, and academic accomplishments in your awards box immediately upon receiving them.

---

*Research Programs That Relate to Your Passions.*

*There are many local, state, national, and international academic and scholarship competitions that reflect a broad range of academic scholarship and student interests.*

*As there are local, state, national, and international competitions in dance and sports, there are programs and competitions that relate to a student's passion in math, science, literature, geography, speech and debate, and other academic areas.*

*[A High School Plan for Students with College-Bound Dreams, p. 103]*

---

# Chapter 6

## *Plan Your Schedule*

After familiarizing yourself with the types of high school diplomas offered in Texas, the amount of academic preparation the colleges you are interested in applying to want to see in their applicants, and the type and level of classes offered at your local middle school and high school, you must develop your seven-year middle school-through-high school schedule accordingly. If you began your college planning in middle school, your high school schedule will represent the final four years of a seven-year schedule. Whether you are only beginning the process of developing your course schedule or need to make adjustments as you experience subjects and levels of coursework, you should plan to discuss or revise your schedule as needed with your counselor or career advisor.

# 24: develop your class schedule

You should carefully and thoughtfully develop a class schedule from today through high school graduation. Important questions to be raised are:

1. Will my elementary school grades or test scores determine the classes I can take in middle school?

2. Are there levels or choices of classes in middle school and how will they influence the classes I may take in high school?

3. Are any middle school classes available for high school credit?

4. Can any high school classes be taken during the summer before entering the ninth grade?

5. Does the school district offer options for taking classes online, during summer school, in night school, or at other schools?

6. What type of high school program do I want to pursue (i.e., Minimum, Recommended, or Distinguished)?

7. How rigorous do I want my course schedule to be (i.e., honors, Pre-AP, AP, dual/joint enrollment)?

8. Am I planning to pursue an athletic scholarship, and if so, what are the NCAA student-athlete eligibility requirements?

9. Am I planning to begin in a Community College or enter directly into a 4-year college or university?

10. What elective classes are available that relate to my areas of interest (e.g., art, music, dance, medicine, or sports law)?

11. Will my class schedule meet the requirements for admission into the colleges I want to attend?

---

# 25: know your options

---

Most people think of summer school as being for students who are struggling. However, consider summer school as an opportunity to take classes that are required for graduation—World History, P.E., Health, electives, etc.—to free your schedule during the school year for additional math, science, language arts, honors, Pre-AP, or AP classes. Classes in summer school may also be used as a means of meeting your graduation requirements by the end of your junior year or the first semester of your senior year. This approach allows for early graduation, early college enrollment, or internship opportunities. Discuss the full range of options with your counselor.

## 26: maximize your options

Night school, community college, or online programs may provide other opportunities to take required, elective, or special-focus classes. Some school districts offer joint or dual enrollment opportunities, online classes, or have agreements with neighboring school districts offering such classes. Many students find the online learning experience an enjoyable and engaging one while other students find it difficult to responsibly manage their time. Talk to your counselor to understand the full range of options and how the grades from such classes will impact your class ranking.

Discuss the array of opportunities with your parents and choose the options that are best for you.

Other options to be considered include:

- Internships
- Independent study
- Taking the school's yearbook class, developing the school's website, or working on the staff of the school newspaper
- Exchange programs with other schools
- Pre-college and after-school programs
- Community service projects
- Working on a political campaign
- Enrolling in an academic or pre-college program
- Attending programs in music, dance, art, or theatre
- After-school jobs that can be designed to become internships like working at a nail salon for entrepreneurial studies, working at a senior citizen home for nursing studies, designing brochures for graphic arts studies, or writing/publishing a book

# 27: 9th grade

Beginning in 9th grade, take the most challenging classes. Whether you experience difficulty making the transition into high school or immediately begin participating in sports, student organizations, and extracurricular activities, you must develop the class schedule that is most appropriate for you. Consider all options when planning your course schedule so you do not overburden yourself. Take a challenging schedule that will prepare you for college and which you believe you can achieve satisfactory grades (generally a 'B' or higher).

The Texas Education Agency currently requires two years of a language other than English for the *Recommended High School Program* and three years for the *Distinguished Achievement Program*. However, you should consider taking a foreign language during each of your four years of high school, culminating in an AP foreign language or Dual

Credit class. If your first language is other than English, consider taking classes in your first language, e.g., Spanish, French, Japanese, Chinese, etc. Not only will this increase your ability to speak and write in multiple languages, it may expand your college options and future career opportunities.

During Spring Break, plan to study for two SAT Subject Tests to be given in May. Pick your two best subjects. Identify a special-interest summer camp, college-bound camp, or summer school program to strengthen or enhance one or more academic areas. Continue reading, writing, and further developing your communication skills. You will also benefit by reviewing an ACT or SAT vocabulary building book. Read newspapers, magazines, novels, and any other material that expands your vocabulary and reading comprehension skills.

# 28: 10th grade

Carefully select among honors and AP classes available to sophomores at your school. However, do not take such a rigorous course schedule that you cannot play a sport, participant in student organizations, extracurricular, or volunteer activities. Colleges will look for students who were academically challenged as well as students who contributed to their school community through sports, student government, extracurricular activities, and community service participation. Try to put yourself on track toward Advanced Placement or Dual Credit classes by 11th and 12th grades, particularly in math and science.

Plan to take the ACT and PSAT (or SAT). All your scores will help to identify your strengths and weaknesses. Remember that your 11th-grade PSAT scores will be used to qualify for National Merit or National Achievement Scholar recognition.

By Spring Break, begin preparing for at least two more SAT Subject Tests. Again, choose your best subjects. Use the summer months to continue strengthening your areas of interests and preparing yourself academically for the challenging classes you plan to take during your junior year. Continue summer camp or summer school opportunities to push yourself academically.

---

## 29: 11th grade

---

Hopefully you will be on track to take a full schedule of the most demanding classes available at your high school during your junior and senior years. Your advanced course schedule should have prepared you to do well on the PSAT, SAT, and ACT. Begin working on your application and financial-aid essays. Perhaps a teacher from an English, language arts, or writing class or a tutor will be willing to critique your essays. Identify any remaining SAT Subject Tests that are required by the colleges on your list. If you have met their requirements, then plan to take two more

SAT Subject Tests in your favorite subjects. Many colleges may require one specific SAT Subject Test and allow you to submit two or three of your choice. You want to submit your highest scores.

## 30: 12th grade

Avoid believing that taking a challenging course load in 9th through 11th grade allows you to take easy classes during your senior year. A bodybuilder would not maintain a healthy diet, five-day-a-week workouts, and extensive cardiovascular training, only to take a year off. One year off may take three years to regain his or her physique, form, and muscular definition. Your rigorous high school schedule has been designed not simply to get you admitted into college, but to succeed once you get there.

# 31: meet with your counselor

Meet with your counselor to ensure that you fully understand the opportunities at your high school. Following, are some questions to assist in guiding your discussions with your high school career or guidance counselor:

1. What are the required and recommended courses— for graduation and for college prep?

2. If I do not qualify for automatic admissions through the Top Ten Percent law, what classes will make me a competitive candidate for all of my top-choice colleges?

3. Which elective courses do you recommend?

4. I have indicated the honors, Pre-AP, AP, and dual credit courses I am interested in taking and I would like to know if there is anything I must do to meet all the prerequisites or enrollment requirements?

5. Can any of my elective or required classes be taken in summer school, night school, online, of for dual credit?

6. Are there tutors or is there a school-sponsored tutorial program you would recommend?

7. What are your thoughts on the four-year schedule that I have developed?

8. When is the PSAT/NMSQT given?

9. Are there any after-school, evening, or special classes available for college planning or SAT/ACT preparation?

10. Do you have practice tests for the SAT, ACT, or STAAR EOC exams?

11. Do you have a college-planning guide or calendar that outlines the types of things I should be doing each year?

12. Is there a list of colleges that have a relationship with or actively recruit from this school?

13. Are there any college fairs at this school or nearby? And, if so, how can I find out when they are scheduled?

14. What are the requirements or standards for the National Honor Society?

15. What clubs, organizations, community service, or student activities do you suggest I consider joining or becoming involved in?

16. I have developed a list of the types of colleges I am interested in applying to. Do you have any information or are there any alumni from our school who can provide me with information about any of the schools on my list?

17. Are there any special scholarships or awards that I should be aware of that I can begin preparing myself?

18. How does our school compare to others, in terms of test scores, reputation, and ranking?

19. What is the deadline for submitting class requests for the next school year?

20. What are the cords, honors, or scholarships awarded to students at our high school graduation ceremony?

# Chapter 7

## *Standardized Testing/EOC Exams*

- **PSAT:** 9th, 10th, 11th grades (October)

- **SAT (also called the SAT Reasoning Test):** Offered several times a year

- **SAT Subject Tests:** Subject tests that you should take close to completing the respective subject

- **ACT:** Offered five times a year

- **AP Exam:** Given in May

- **STARR EOC:** The state of Texas requires 12 end-of-course (EOC) assessments for public high school students in: Algebra I, geometry, Algebra II, biology, chemistry, physics, English I, English II, English III, world geography, world history, and U.S. history

# 32: SAT/ACT prep

If you are planning to apply to a college that requires that you submit SAT or ACT scores (*visit www.fairtest.org for a listing of colleges not requiring SAT or ACT scores*), avoid two common mistakes that many students make—they do not effectively prepare for the SAT or ACT, and, they wait until senior year to take them. As soon as you are prepared to take the SAT or ACT, take them. Allow yourself enough time to retake them should you want to increase your scores.

College admissions committees must eliminate applications to get to the right class size. Many colleges will eliminate thousands of applications to arrive at a class size of a few hundred students. Standardized test scores provide admissions committees with an easy way to eliminate applications.

- If your school offers a test preparation class, take it.
- If your school does not offer a class, find a free class at a local public library, church, YMCA, or Boys and Girls Club.

- If you cannot find a free class, find one that you can afford being offered by one of the private companies.
- If you cannot find a free class and you cannot afford to pay for one, pick up a test preparation book at the bookstore or local library and go onto the Internet and do a search for "SAT/ACT practice tests" and prepare yourself.

Take the SAT or ACT as early as your sophomore year—certainly by your junior year—to determine whether or not your scores qualify for admission into the colleges on your list or the scholarships you will be applying for. If you are not satisfied with your scores, consider taking the test again, concentrating on the section (e.g., critical reading and writing, or math) where you would most like to improve your score. Most colleges that require SAT or ACT scores will accept the highest score for each section, even if the scores occurred on different testing dates.

While the tests are attempting to assess your academic abilities and preparation for college, the best preparation is to work hard and take rigorous middle school and high school classes. However, it would be advisable to engage in a thorough review of math fundamentals and vocabulary prior to taking the ACT or SAT.

# 33: know the tests

## ACT (a perfect score is 36)

The ACT (American College Testing Exam) is a national college admission examination that tests students' knowledge in four subject areas and an optional Writing section. The tests, and scores considered to demonstrate college readiness, are: English (18); Mathematics (22); Reading (21); and Science (24).

ACT results are accepted by virtually all U.S. colleges and universities. The ACT includes 215 multiple-choice questions and takes approximately three hours and 30 minutes to complete with breaks.

**Your score is based on the number of correct answers only, so if you are not sure, taking a guess does not hurt.**

## PSAT (a perfect score is 80)

The PSAT (Preliminary SAT) consists of two 25-minute critical reading sections, two 25-minute math sections, and one 30-minute writing skills section. The PSAT provides practice for the SAT, an evaluation of your abilities in comparison with other college-bound students, an opportunity to enter scholarship competitions, a chance to learn about colleges interested in students with a profile similar to yours, and may qualify you for *National Merit* and *National Achievement* scholarship consideration.

As a result of your answers to the PSAT questionnaire, you may begin receiving information in the mail from interested colleges so be sure to answer the questions carefully and provide an accurate mailing address. The PSAT score range is between 20 and 80.

**Junior-year scores are used to determine qualification for the National Merit and National Achievement Scholar programs.**

## SAT (a perfect score is 2400)

The first SAT (Scholastic Aptitude Test, now referred to as the Scholastic Assessment Test) was administered in 1926 to 8,040 students. Today more than two million students annually take the SAT. The most recent change to the SAT occurred in 2005. The verbal section was replaced with the writing and critical reading sections. The current SAT consists of 3 sections with a maximum score of 800 in each section.

The writing section consists of a 35-minute multiple-choice section and a 25-minute essay. The critical reading section consists of two 25-minute and one 20-minute sections. The math section consists of two 25-minute and one 20-minute sections. National testing dates occur during October, November, December, January, March, May, and June.

**The SAT carries a wrong answer penalty (either 1/4 or 1/3 point) with no deduction for blank answers.**

## SAT Subject Tests (a perfect score is 800)

The SAT Subject Tests consists of tests offered in five subject areas (English, history, mathematics, science, and foreign languages) that are one-hour, mostly multiple-choice tests, designed to measure how much students know about a particular academic subject and how well they can apply that knowledge. Colleges use the test scores primarily for class placement; however, up to three tests may be required for some college admissions. The SAT Subject Tests are offered during October, November, December, January, May, and June.

## CLEP (College-Level Examination Program)

CLEP is the College-Level Examination Program that provides students with the opportunity to demonstrate college-level achievement through a program of exams in undergraduate college courses. There are 2,900 colleges that grant credit or advanced standing for CLEP exams. Each college publishes its qualifying criteria and number of credits awarded. The qualifying criteria and credits awarded will vary by college.

# Chapter 8

## *Extracurricular Activities*

Many of the country's top students, with top grades and top SAT/ACT scores, do not get admitted into their first-choice colleges. Unfortunately, many of the top students are working so hard academically they cannot find time to become involved in their school or community. It seems unfair that colleges want both scholarly students and students who are well rounded as a result of their athletic, extracurricular activities, or community service involvement. However, that is exactly what they want.

There is no perfect GPA, SAT/ACT scores, and extracurricular activity balance. Therefore, live your life! Play the sports you enjoy, become involved in those student organizations that reflect your passions and interests, and perform community service because it is the right thing to do! College admissions officers are likely to value your passion, compassion, and contributions to your school or community.

## 34: make a contribution

As you explore the wide range of extracurricular activities available, both at your high school and within community, civic, or clerical organizations, pay special attention to opportunities that can eventually lead to scholarship consideration. The obvious possibilities relate to athletics; however, there are many not-so-obvious opportunities that increase your chances of receiving a wide range of scholarship awards.

- Student Government
- Creative/Performing Arts
- Science/Research Projects
- Boy and Girl Scouts
- Future Business Leaders

- Community Service
- Speech and Debate
- Faith-based Programs
- Junior Achievement
- Junior ROTC

# 35: do something noteworthy

Academic preparation and standardized test scores have been covered in great detail because they undoubtedly are at the top of your stat sheet. They are the first things the admissions officer will see and oftentimes will determine whether or not your application is rejected outright before he or she has had an opportunity to get to know who you are and the contribution you can make to his or her college community. If you make the first cut, your application will then be in a pile among hundreds, if not thousands, of other applications from students who are also academically qualified. It is at this point that who you are, what your interests are, and what contribution you can make to the college during your four years there and in society afterwards, will influence whether or not you are admitted.

- Sports
- Community Service
- Clubs
- Volunteer Hours
- Student Organizations
- Work Experience

True leadership, is not reflected in how many offices you hold or the number of organizations you can claim membership, but by who you are and how your school, family, friends, and community have benefited from your skills, talents, gifts, abilities, and compassion. School districts spend huge amounts of money teaching character values to elementary and middle school students; however, as a high school student, you have the choice of standing for something or falling for anything. If your friends encourage rebellion against your parents or mean-spirited behavior toward other students, your choices will define who you are—a sheep in the herd or the shepherd of the herd, a goose on a mindless migration or an eagle soaring high above the clouds. There is no substitute for character and true leadership always reveals itself.

Admissions officers are interested in not only that you played a sport, but that you were willing to accept the responsibility of being the captain or co-captain of the team, organized a study hall, tutored other players, or encouraged teammates to focus on their academic preparation with the same passion as they prepared for athletic competition. An admissions officer is interested in not only that you belonged to organizations but that your involvement resulted in meaningful contributions through innovation, creativity, and collaboration. When you submit your college essays and you are asked for words that describe your character, you will want such words as duty, integrity, resilient, self-motivated, willing to collaborate, responsible, and respectful to define who you are.

## 36: be involved in activities

Identify the full range of extracurricular activities (i.e., JROTC, sports, clubs, organizations, community service, etc.) available at your high school and pick at least two you are willing to commit to for four years. Colleges are interested in the *commitment* and *contribution* to your activities. The greater the number of years you demonstrate involvement in a particular activity, the more supportive it will be of your overall college application.

If some of the schools on your list have highly-competitive admissions standards, then do some research and identify the clubs, student activities, or student organizations that are important to each school. Join one of the clubs or student organizations that would be highly thought of at your first-choice college and plan to highlight your involvement on your application, in your essay, or during your interview. Also, join another club or participate in an activity that you will enjoy and make a contribution that can be mentioned prominently on your college application and in your personal biography.

## 37: perform community service

Consider your personal areas of interest and identify a community service project of value to your community or a community organization where you can volunteer. Consider the question, "How can I do what I enjoy and use it to benefit my country, church, school, or community?"

# 38: consider a sport

Athletics is one of the important parts of the college experience. Interest by a college coach for an intercollegiate sport or by an admissions committee for your potential contribution to the school's intramural sports programs may have a significant impact on your admissions status. If you have athletic abilities, you should consider developing them as a means of helping you to gain college admission or possibly receiving a full or partial scholarship to offset the costs of college tuition, fees, room, and board.

Set yourself apart from other athletes. Consider less popular sports like golf, tennis, water polo, Judo, rowing, and fencing. Colleges oftentimes recruit scholarship athletes from outside of the United States, due to low interest in these types of sports by American high school students.

Choosing a club, organization, or student activity should reflect your interest and enhance your college plan.

# 39:  consider clubs and band

Just because a club or organization does not have much student interest at your high school does not mean that your involvement will not generate interest from colleges. For example, if the student government at your high school does not generate much student interest, your becoming involved and assuming a leadership position is impressive on your college application, even if it is not highly thought of in your high school. Any time there is a weak club or organization that does not generate a lot of student interest, you should see it as an opportunity. If you can revitalize a student activity or organization at your high school, church, or community organization, you will have a powerful story to tell on your college or scholarship essay and to share during a college interview.

Even if you are currently attending elementary school, identify all the clubs and student organizations available at your high school, even those that you may not be interested in, at this time. It will be your high school involvement in activities and community service that will be reflected on your résumé and your college applications. As you move forward with developing your college plan, you may find that becoming involved in some of the clubs or organizations that you may not be interested in at this time may be important to helping you to be accepted into the college of your choice.

Playing a musical instrument and being a member of a successful marching band may provide more scholarship opportunities than being a varsity athlete. Many colleges not only award music scholarships, but have stronger band traditions than they do athletic traditions and may actively recruit band members and award many band scholarships. Instruments such as the Bassoon, English Horn, Oboe, and Harp may provide students with unique scholarship opportunities.

# 40: community involvement

Mentoring or tutoring at a community center, maintaining the website for a local organization, updating Facebook pages for a political campaign, designing sets for a local theatre, taking photographs for a community newspaper, coaching youth sports, rasing money for charities, collecting clothes or toiletries for homeless shelters, reading to students at local schools, or raising community awareness about social, health, or environmental issues, all provide opportunities to enhance your college application and make a positive contribution to your community. These kinds of involvement also provide opportunities to be formally recognized by organizations and the news media (another way of enhancing your college application).

Make a list of the programs and activities, which you are currently involved or have an interest in becoming involved. Keep in mind that there is always an opportunity for you to work with others to begin a new program.

# 41: competitions

Competitions provide additional opportunities to earn scholarship money. Successfully competing in local and national competitions may further enhance your college application. Competitions are available a broad range of student-interest areas such areas as sports, music, academics, the arts, debating, and robotics. Begin identifying the competitions you may be interested in entering. Keep track of your participation and any awards you receive.

# 42: get a job

Carefully consider available job opportunities. Instead of merely bagging groceries, explore employment opportunities within areas of interest or areas that provide practical applications for some of your coursework. You may even need to consider one paid job, like bagging groceries, and one unpaid job or internship that relates to classes that you have been taking in school such as:

- *Word Processing:* Secretarial, office assistant, general office, data entry

- *Art:* Flyers, store window themes, brochures, signs, t-shirts, and web page design

- *Weight Training:* Assisting personal trainers, stacking weights at a health club

- *Speech & Debate:* Sales, telemarketing, customer service

- *English Language Arts:* Editing, proof reading, writing a blog or newsletter, responding to letters in a political campaign office

- *Math:* Accounting, tax preparation assistance, bookkeeping

- *Science:* Veterinarian's office, dental office, drug-store sales

- *Music:* Recording studio, store selling/repairing musical instruments

- *Culinary Arts:* Being a chef's assistant, restaurant, catering service

# Chapter 9

## *Personal Qualities*

No matter how you compare to others in terms of grades and test scores, who you are, what you have done, and what you stand for can become the defining factor that convinces an admissions officer that you are a student who would make a noteworthy contribution to his or her college community. From the time you begin kindergarten, each day will provide the opportunity to separate from the masses and define yourself. More than trying to make yourself into something, allow the divinely unique person whom you were created to be to come to the surface. Do not try to blend in and be like everyone else. Allow the divinely unique you to blossom. Not only will you distinguish yourself from the thousands of other applicants, but you will more likely identify the college community that would provide the best environment to nurture your artistic, personal, intellectual, and spiritual growth.

# 43: be a leader

Colleges are looking for leaders—students who can contribute to intellectual discussions, challenge professors, create music, explore science, and provide creative and intellectual insight into the issues of today and contribute to their communities.

Have you been maximizing your leadership opportunities?

- Have you contributed to the creation of a new student club or organization?

- Have you been elected into office or served in a leadership capacity in an organization?

- Have you made a meaningful contribution to your school or community?

- Have you created a new approach or implemented a new way of doing things that has enhanced your school, church, or community?

- Have you taught, tutored, coached, inspired, or encouraged others?

- Have you taken something that you have learned through a classroom experience and applied it through the creation of a new product or new way of doing things?

- Have you led a social cause or publicly lobbied for a legislative change?

## 44: define your character

Your character defines who you are, what you stand for, and the beliefs and principles that guide your life. Do not allow yourself to be influenced by mean-spirited, self-centered, obnoxious people who go out of their way to ridicule, take advantage of, and hinder others. Do not follow the crowd or allow such people to define your character.

What are your values, beliefs, and guiding principles? Take a moment and write down five values that define who you are. Ultimately, a person will be known by his or her works. If these values truly define who you are today, then they will be evident in your works by the time you write your college and scholarship essays.

Many colleges will require teacher recommendations. Teachers will be asked to share their comments and insight into your personality and academic abilities. Some colleges will provide teachers with a checklist to rate such qualities as:

- personality
- curiosity
- academic promise
- self-confidence
- warmth of personality
- concern for others

# 45: get to know 3 teachers

Over the course of your four years of high school, take the time to get to know at least three teachers—people who would value the opportunity to write a letter telling the world what a wonderful person you are and attesting to your character and academic abilities. Your participation in classroom discussions, contribution to group projects, and involvement in clubs and student organizations will provide many opportunities to develop relationships and for teachers to form an opinion about your character and to develop an honest assessment of your academic abilities.

Admissions officers will view your involvement in your high school as indicative of your potential involvement in the vibrant life of their college community, which will offer an even broader range of clubs and organizations. Developing good relationships with your high school teachers will be good preparation for developing such relationships with your college professors.

# 46: avoid discipline violations

To take full advantage of the range of high school opportunities, you have to take your school's policies, procedures, and code of conduct seriously. Discipline infractions not only disrupt the high school experience for classmates, interfere with classroom instruction, and contribute negatively to your school's overall school climate and culture but may cause you to forfeit your opportunity to participate in extracurricular activities, student organizations, or keep you from being recommended for programs and awards that would otherwise enhance your college application package.

Your high school record may contain a complete listing of your discipline infractions for each year of high school. You do not want a code of conduct or discipline violation in the ninth grade to hinder your college application in the twelfth grade.

# Chapter 10

## *Intangibles*

Intangibles represent all of those areas not previously covered, which contribute to your uniqueness:

- Where you live

- Ethnicity, gender, and family structure

- Legacy status (i.e., one of your parents graduated from the college you are applying to)

- Experiences and circumstances

Your geographical area and community setting will have an impact on your application. Many colleges seek to develop a diverse freshman class of students from different geographical regions—throughout the United States and other countries, and types of communities—urban, suburban, rural, liberal, conservative, etc. While in-state tuition is usually substantially less at public universities than out-of-state tuition, you may be more easily accepted to an out-of-state college looking for students from your geographical region who may also offer you a financial-aid package that meets your needs.

## 47: understand your competition

While many public universities lack socioeconomic and cultural diversity, other colleges may have admissions criteria that places a high value on geographical, socioeconomic, racial, or gender diversity. If you are from an affluent background, you may have more competition being accepted into some of the top schools where large numbers of students from similar socioeconomic backgrounds apply. However, a student from a working class or poor family may be among only a few applicants from similar socioeconomic backgrounds.

The very life experiences that may create huge barriers for students, may be the experiences that give students a huge advantage in the college admissions process. For example, a student from a migrant family who is forced to move frequently and enroll into a number of schools and school districts has a very different educational experience than a student from a middle class family of professional parents in a stable home environment. If both students take similar classes, and achieve comparable grades and test scores, the student from the migrant family clearly will have done so while having to overcome a more difficult set of circumstances than the student from the middle class family. This may give the migrant student favorable consideration in the admissions process.

The question you must ask is, "If there are a large number of applications from students who have a similar ethnic, socioeconomic, and family background as myself, what can I do to distinguish myself?" Also consider the number of students, like yourself, competing for the limited number of scholarships offered by the colleges and universities on your list.

# 48: celebrate your experiences

Your experiences, such as where you have traveled, the type of communities where you have lived, the organizations you have been involved with, and programs or camps in which you have participated contribute to your intangibles. Your family experiences have uniquely contributed to who you are, whether your parents are millionaires or migrant workers, serving in law enforcement or in a political office, delivering mail or delivering babies, researching environmental issues or performing landscaping, teaching students in regular classrooms or prison inmates, or serving children in school cafeterias or serving in the military. The uniqueness of your family background provides the substance of your hopes, dreams, perspective, and perception of the world around you. Whether from privilege or from the projects, there is no shame in your unique background and experiences; all geographical areas, ethnicity, and socioeconomic backgrounds reflect the diversity of the global landscape.

# 49: choose the right college

Beyond size, location, and national ranking, identify colleges with a strong department in the area in which you want to study and with professors who can assist you in pursuing your passions through their classes and programs. Are you passionate about engineering and technology? Do you compose and perform music? Are you passionate about theatre? Are you fascinated with science? Are you passionate about politics or social justice? Do you find joy in writing poetry, stories, or screen plays? Do you have unique gifts in drawing or painting? Are you passionate about film or photography? Not only will your passions and areas of interest direct your college research and identify potential college majors, your dreams and aspirations will separate your application from the masses. The right college will want you as much as you will want to become a student!

Your areas of interest may expand your college opportunities. For example, fewer African American and Hispanic students are interested in pursuing STEM-related majors (i.e., Science, Technology, Engineering, and Mathematics). Subsequently, such students may find themselves more aggressively recruited than students interested in pursuing college majors in other areas. Students who are interested in pursing such areas as music and art and who have demonstrated a passion in these areas extending back to elementary school may have an advantage over students who say they are interested in pursing music or art but took their first art class as a high school senior.

---

# 50: plan your summers

---

Identify opportunities during the summer months between 8th grade and your senior year of high school to expand your academic skills, develop your gifts and talents, and broaden your experiences. Take advantage of opportunities to develop your musical, athletic, or artistic talents. Some of the many opportunities you may explore, experience, or become involved in are:

- Traveling
- Working in a meaningful job related to an area of interest or participating in an internship
- Participating in a summer learning opportunity in an academic, artistic, community service, or leadership area
- Participating in pre-college summer camps/programs
- Participating in an AAU (Amateur Athletic Union), USATF (USA Track & Field), or club sport
- Participating in summer practice for a high school sport such as football, cross country, lacrosse, soccer, swimming, etc.
- Volunteering as a counselor, life guard, coach, or art instructor at a parks and recreation, Boys and Girls Club, or community program
- Taking some of your non-academic classes or electives in summer school to open your schedule for more honors, Pre-AP (Advanced Placement), AP, or dual credit classes during the regular school year
- Starting a business or working on a special project

Unlike the summer months during elementary and middle school, this is not the time to relax at grandma's house sitting back and watching television or playing video games. The summer months provide opportunities to work, attend camps or summer school, compete in athletic competitions, participate in internships, or otherwise engage in programs or opportunities that will expand your gifts, talents, skills, and academic abilities.

## 51: attend a camp or internship

There are many summer enrichment, internship, and pre-college program opportunities. The first two stops are your high school counselor's office and the Internet. Research programs related to your areas of interest and utilize the opportunity to increase your academic, athletic, creative, or work skills. Try to concentrate first and foremost on those areas that relate directly to your college interests, whether in your major field of study or in sports you intend to pursue on the college level.

# Chapter 11

## *Your Essay*

Do not take your essays lightly; they may represent the most important part of your college application package and may even earn you thousands of dollars in college scholarship money. Each essay provides you with the opportunity to define who you are and state your case for admission into the college or for a college scholarship. Your essay can take away from or enhance the overall picture of who you are, what you stand for, and why the admissions or scholarship committee should give you an opportunity ahead of the thousands of other applicants. This is your opportunity to explain your grades; share your convictions, beliefs, philosophies, and guiding principles; tell what you know about the college's or scholarship committee's values, beliefs, and traditions; and merge your hopes, dreams, and aspirations. Some college admissions and scholarship committees use noncognitive variables to assess your essay. These variables are: self-concept; realistic self-appraisal; handling system/racism; long-range goals; leadership; strong support person; community; and nontraditional learning. Ask your teacher or counselor for assistance in ensuring that as many of these variables as possible are reflected in your essays.

Imagine your essay standing on a stage. The curtain pulls back and your essay walks from center stage to the podium. The spotlight shines, but there is talking and lack of interest throughout the room as thousands of other essays whisper, motion, and scream for attention, yet it is your essay standing alone at the podium as a Sunday morning preacher.

> *"I ain't where I wanna be,*
>
> > *I ain't where I oughta be,*
> > *I ain't where I need to be,*
> *But thank God,*
> > *I ain't where I was."*

There is silence throughout the auditorium as all voices and distractions quiet. All discourse, debate, and discussions become still as a lake beneath the moonlight, as your essay captures, captivates, and continues a brilliant oratory on your behalf—sharing your hopes and your dreams, your achievements and your aspirations, your frailties and your uniqueness—your essay is the single ripple on the water carrying your message as the ripples widen and spread into the spirit, soul, and consciousness of the listener.

# 52: practice, practice, practice

An important part of the process of preparing and practicing requires that you read other essays. What you learn from reading good essays and bad essays can help you to create a great essay. Your goal from the beginning must be to create a great essay—not merely a good one but a best seller—one that will leave a lasting impression. The essay is such an important component of your college admissions and scholarship application that you should not wait until the last minute to begin writing. Good essays are written months, if not years, in advance.

1. Practice.

2. Read other essays.

3. Read as many essay-preparation books as you need in order to understand the essay-writing process.

4. Write essays for extra credit throughout middle and high school and allow your teachers to assist with editing, grammar, punctuation, style, and content.

5. Keep in mind the basic admissions officer's question, "What does this applicant offer our college?"

## 53: tell your story

The sooner you begin to assess your life based on some of the important essay themes, the faster you will begin to explore the important things about yourself and your character, the obstacles you have had to overcome and what makes you uniquely the person you are. A good essay written along the following themes can make a lasting impression on the readers of your essay:

- Hard work
- Overcoming obstacles
- Being of service
- Teamwork
- Perseverance
- Individual initiative
- Passion and enthusiasm
- Responsibility
- Civic duty
- Purpose
- Character or core value
- Autobiography
- Person you most admire
- Major challenge in your life
- Something significant that you want to accomplish
- Your strengths and weaknesses
- An issue of personal, local, national, or international concern
- Actions you would take if you were in a position of leadership, e.g., politician, principal, CEO, etc.
- Stories of leadership, personal sacrifice, or service that have inspired you

# 54: identify your heroes/heroines

- What people have demonstrated, through their lives or their ability to overcome obstacles, an example that you wish to follow?

- What people have left a legacy that has provided an example of the values that humanity should aspire toward?

- What people embody the values, beliefs, and ideals that define who you are or what you aspire to become?

- What people have, through their thoughts, words, or deeds, changed the course of human history in a meaningful and relevant way?

- With which historical figures would you value the opportunity to sit and discuss ideas, opinions, and views on the most pressing social or political issues of the day?

Make a list of the people whom you most admire in such areas as:

- Family or community
- Historical figures
- Political, civic, business, or religious leaders
- Educators (i.e., teachers, counselors, administrators, or coaches)
- Athletes, entertainers, and public figures
- Everyday people, e.g., custodians, cafeteria workers, farmers, brick masons, waiters or waitresses

## 55: get help

The reason you want to begin experimenting with your essay writing in your early years of middle and high school is that it is an important skill to develop. You will benefit, for not only your college applications and scholarship submissions, but, for the reading and writing components of the PSAT, SAT, and ACT as well as preparation for the writing component of high school end-of-course exams.

This is your future. You must passionately share your story. It does not matter how well or badly written the first drafts of your essays are. Ask your English, language arts, and literature teachers to edit, critique, and provide feedback on your grammar, style, and voice. You may even be able to earn extra credit for some of your writing. The way to become good at writing is to write often and to develop a willingness to accept constructive criticism.

## 56: carefully choose your words

Passion • Purpose • Perseverance • Compassion • Integrity • Diligence • Respect • Responsibility • Determination • Persistence • Dedication • Devotion • Commitment • Enthusiasm • Energy • Fortitude • Kindness • Humanity • Generosity • Selflessness • Tolerance • Awareness • Service • Sense of duty • Leadership • Teamwork • Cooperation • Humor • Originality • Innovation • Imagination • Thoughtful • Judgment • Independence • Honor • Morality • Resilience • Experimentation • Idealism • Vision •

Mission • Conceptualized • Created • Explored • Pursued •
Discovered • Developed • Taught • Trained • Coached • Led
• Reformed • Established • Initiated • Tutored • Founded
• Felt obligated • Collaborated with • Entrepreneurship •
Was responsible for

---

# 57: create a quality essay

---

Do not just sit down and start writing. Take the time
to prepare yourself mentally and identify the necessary
resources to develop a well-thought-out and well-written
essay. When your essay steps to the podium, you do not
want a hair out of place, food between his or her teeth, mud
on his or her shoes, her slip showing, or his fly opened! You
do not want anything to take away from the oratory. When
you submit your essay, make it the best and highest quality.
You will not be there to explain errors, mistakes, smudges,
stains, or anything that will distract the reader from reading
your story and getting to know your hopes and your

dreams. Before you submit your essay, find the person who never likes anything that you do—the one person who is always critical—and allow him or her to read your essay to see if he or she can find anything wrong. Invite the person to "let you have it," to be as critical as possible. If you can win him or her over, you are on your way to submitting an outstanding essay.

Although previously stated, the point bears repeating that you should write your essay days, weeks, or even months in advance so you can read it, have someone else read it, have a teacher proof it, and then read it again. Please remember that "spell checking" a computer document is not enough as the computer may substitute or overlook misused words. Even after all the reading, you may find "if" when you meant "of" or "and" when you meant "an" or "he" when you meant "the." As a final check, read your essay aloud, count the number of words, and review the scholarship or college application guidelines!

# Chapter 12

## *Financial Aid/Scholarships*

Acquiring the needed financial aid to pay for the cost of college will require that you determine the best strategy based on your family's financial situation and the type and amount of financial aid available at the colleges to which you will be applying. Begin your scholarship research by gathering information from the following websites:

- Every Chance Every Texan: *www.everychanceeverytexan.org*

- College for All Texans: *www.collegeforalltexans.com*

- Texas Financial Aid Information Center: *www.tgslc.org*

Carefully and thoroughly identify the financial aid options at the colleges or universities you are interested in applying to, the qualifications for financial aid, and the deadlines to apply. If you have the time, there are literally hundreds of scholarships that you can research and apply to. If you do not have the time, then you must focus your attention on identifying the colleges that will provide the necessary financial aid through institutional scholarships and grants. The 3-step approach you might consider is:

1. Identify the colleges that can offer you most, if not all of the financial aid that you need (without loans).

2. Identify the scholarships that can provide the balance of what you need so that you do not have to take out any loans.

3. If you must take out a loan, do not exceed the federal subsidized loan limit.

## 58: set aside two boxes

- One box for the scholarships that you apply to which will contain your essays and necessary application information

- The second box for your overflow of scholarship information that you may not be considering at this time

# 59: start early

It is important to start early so that you apply for the right scholarships, apply to the right colleges, and complete the FAFSA (Free Application for Federal Student Aid) by the necessary deadlines.

# 60: get a permanent address

Once you begin applying for scholarships, your name and address will find its way onto many different mailing lists and into many different scholarship databases. You are going to begin receiving lots of mail. Try to get a stable mailing address and consistent e-mail address. Our sons use our P.O. Box and business e-mail address for all of their college and scholarship applications. Otherwise, we could have used my mother's address. She has lived at the same address for over 30 years. Do not run the risk of missing out on a big scholarship award because it was sent to the wrong address.

# 61: get a high speed connection

There are more scholarships available on the web—more information and applications that can be downloaded than you will ever have the time to research. You will need access to a high-speed Internet connection, i.e., DSL, Cable, Satellite, etc. If you need to access the Internet from a computer at your school or from the public library, get a flash drive so that you can download files and always have your essays, résumé, college applications, and scholarship information with you.

# 62: organize your paperwork

Get your essays and paperwork together. Most scholarships only require that you complete an application, write an essay, include some paperwork, and submit the package by the deadline. Keep all of your original documents filed neatly in a box and keep copies in a binder under the appropriate tabs like grades, test scores, transcript, letters of recommendation, financial records, awards, essays, summaries of your extracurricular activities, etc.

## 63: organize your financial info

There are some mandatory forms that you must complete so now is a good time to become familiar with the financial aid information required to complete the forms. The experience will also help you to understand what information—tax forms, social security numbers, employment income, assets, liabilities, etc.,—is going to be required. If you or your parents treasure your privacy, then you are about to discover that your financial life is going to become an open book. The most important thing for you to keep in mind is do not guess. Also, do not lie! Gather all of the required information and answer all of the questions truthfully.

1. Get a copy of the *Common Application* at *www. commonapp.org/* and complete it fully. The information that you provide on the Common Application will be referred to as you complete the many scholarship applications over the next four years.

2. Get a copy of the *FAFSA* (Free Application for Federal Student Aid) at *www.fafsa.ed.gov/* and complete it fully. This is the application that the federal government and your college will use to determine your eligibility for financial aid and the amount of aid that you are able to receive.

3. Submit your *FAFSA* as soon as possible after January 1 of your senior year. Expect to receive a SAR (Student Aid Report) in about four to six weeks after submitting your FAFSA. THIS WILL BECOME YOUR MOST IMPORTANT FINANCIAL-AID DOCUMENT— DO NOT LOSE IT! NO COLLEGES AND MOST SCHOLARSHIPS WILL NOT AWARD MONEY UNLESS YOU HAVE COMPLETED THE FAFSA.

4. Get a copy of *Funding Your Education*, a free publication from the U.S. Department of Education at *www. studentaid.ed.gov*. From the web site you can also

set up a student financial-aid web account to assist in developing your financial-aid plan based on your current year in school.

5. Contact the financial-aid office at each of the colleges you are interested in applying to and request information on their financial-aid policies and available scholarship programs.

# 64: identify your niche

While you should apply for all types of general scholarships, identify the areas in which you uniquely qualify. Do you, for example, have special interests—art, website design, animation, film, drama, poetry, short stories, journalism, photography, etc.? Belong to a particular ethic group? Low income? Is anyone in your family a member of a particular religious group, professional organization, fraternity, sorority, or fraternal organization like the Masons or Shriners? Are you an athlete? Have you volunteered at the YMCA, Boys and Girls Club, recreation programs, community organizations, or at your church?

Some of the readily identifiable niches are:

- Gender
- Ethnicity
- Disability
- Employment, hobbies, activities
- Competitions, i.e., talent shows, art, dance, etc.
- Religious Affiliation
- Organizational Affiliation
- Community Groups
- Local Businesses
- Local Dollars for Scholars Chapter
- Local Financial Institutions
- Family Affiliation
- College-Career Goals
- Geographical Region
- Merit Qualification (i.e., grades and test scores)
- Service

# 65: get to know your counselor

Although getting to know your counselor could easily have been the first strategy in the book, by now your conversations with your counselor will be much more engaging. Counselors deal with a lot of students and have a great deal of responsibility. By now you should be well prepared with questions and information so that you can maximize the counselor's time and expertise in assisting you in pursuing your college/career aspirations. Let your counselor know that you want to apply for scholarships, you appreciate any information he or she can share with you, and that you will complete the applications and write any necessary essays. Whenever you are awarded a *scholarship*, let your counselor know how much you received and how much you appreciate his or her guidance. This sharing will help you to develop a relationship with your counselor whom you may also have to ask for a letter of recommendation.

# Chapter 13

## *Your Application Package*

Your application package represents the final steps in preparing for and getting accepted into the college of your choice. There is a scripture in the Holy Bible in the Book of Galatians [Chapter 6, verses 4-7]:

> *But let every man prove his own work, and then shall he have rejoicing in himself alone, and not in another. For every man shall bear his own burden ... for whatsoever a man soweth, that shall he also reap."*

As you put together your application package you will see what you have sown in the areas of:

- academics, standardized test scores, academic awards;
- extracurricular activities and community service;
- personal qualities; and
- intangibles.

100

What you have sown will determine the strength of your application package, which will influence the college admissions cycle that you choose to use. Some of the groups in which you may find yourself include:

- *Academic Superstar:* Your grades, coursework, and standardized test scores have elevated you to the level of "Academic Superstar." You may have received a number of merit-based scholarships and find yourself a recruited student who has many college options. Hopefully, one or more of your options are schools that you have noted on your list.

- *Recruited-athlete:* Your success within one or more varsity sports has qualified you as a recruited-athlete. You may have already received offers via the National Letter of Intent program and now find yourself going through the difficult task of evaluating schools and offers. Hopefully, you have received scholarship offers from some of the schools on your list or are in a position to use offer letters from other schools to negotiate a financial-aid package with the schools on your list.

- *Strong Candidate:* The success you have achieved within one or more of the areas (i.e., academics, extracurricular activities, etc.), makes you a strong candidate for admissions. While your acceptance is not guaranteed, you may feel that you are a strong enough candidate who is likely to receive enough acceptance letters that you will be able to compare financial-aid packages prior to committing to a particular college.

- *Legacy Student:* Regardless of whether you are an academic superstar, recruited-athlete, or strong candidate you have made up your mind and are committed to apply under the guidelines as a legacy applicant.

- *Weak Candidate:* After reviewing your application package, you realize that you are not a standout student in any area. However, if you are serious about going to college, then you, more than any other student, will have to do some research. Identify schools where you meet their minimum requirements, particularly schools with open admissions policies, and you must take the time to put together a quality application package and meet all of their posted deadlines. NO EXCEPTIONS!

# 66: decide when to apply

The admissions cycle you choose to submit your application should reflect your situation, i.e., academic superstar, legacy student, weak candidate, etc. Sit down with your parents, mentor, or high school counselor to identify the admissions cycle that is best for you. Once you have made your decision, focus all your attention on creating quality application packages and meeting each college's posted deadlines.

**Early Decision:** This program is offered by approximately 270 colleges and is utilized by students who are absolutely certain of their first-choice school by the beginning of their senior year. Many colleges have higher admission rates for Early Decision applications.

**Early Decision II:** This program has the same restrictions as the Early Decision program. It is offered, by some schools, as a second round of Early Decision that has a later deadline than Early Decision (usually a January deadline).

**Early Action:** This program works like Early Decision, but is not binding and students are not obligated to attend the school if accepted. Students typically receive a response to their application ahead of regular decision applicants.

**Single-Choice Early Action:** This program works like a combination of Early Action and Early Decision. Like Early Action, students are not obligated to attend the school if accepted; however, like Early Decision, students may only apply to one school under the Early Action program.

**Regular Admissions:** The standard admissions evaluation cycle requires submission of your application by a deadline (usually in early to mid-January of the year in which you want to attend college). All applications received by the college are held until the deadline date and all applications are reviewed together. Late applications are reviewed AFTER the review of all applications received by the announced deadline.

**Rolling Admissions:** This evaluation cycle allows applications to be reviewed and decided upon as they arrive in the admissions office. It is best to get your application in as soon as possible after the announcement of the opening of the admissions cycle.

## 67: avoid common mistakes

Avoid such common mistakes as:

- contacting counselors too late to meet application deadlines;
- not filing your FAFSA in a timely manner;
- contacting the college admissions office so late that the majority of financial aid has already been committed to other students;
- failing to take the SAT/ACT until the spring of your senior year;
- not filing for Early Admission to your first-choice school;
- not taking the required SAT Subject Tests required by your first-choice schools; or
- submitting incomplete applications or financial-aid forms.

Keep a sharp lookout for these stumbling blocks:

- Submit the correct number of essays. If the instructions state "choose one," select only one of the suggested essay topics.

- If the instructions state "complete all," write an essay for every topic requested.

- If an essay question has more than one section, provide an answer for every part. Make sure that your responses answer the questions—and make clear which response goes with which question.

- Compute the grade point average according to the instructions. Different schools use different methods for computing GPAs.

- Be careful not to confuse "country" with "county."

- Incorrectly listing the current year for your birthday (e.g. 1/1/03 instead of 1/1/88).

- Writing down the incorrect school name (e.g., Texas A&M instead of Texas Tech, or Baylor instead of Rice).

- Using "white out" or crossing an answer out. Do not undermine all your hard work because you were too busy, too anxious, too negligent, too sloppy, or simply too rushed to take the time to submit a complete, thorough, and quality application.

- Not following instructions
- Repeating yourself
- Spending too much time describing ordinary accomplishments instead of highlighting extraordinary achievements (or failing to recognize your extraordinary achievements)
- Writing down an incorrect home address

Incorrect word usage:
- *if* instead of *of*
- *an* instead of *and*
- *no* instead of *know*
- *from* instead of *form*
- *to* instead of *too*
- *though* instead of *through*
- *chose* instead of *choose*
- *whose* instead of *who's*

# 68: talk to your counselor

Different high schools have different policies and procedures regarding how they would like students to prepare their college application packages. Check with your counselor for the specific guidelines for your high school. Following is a checklist that would satisfy most high school counselors.

- ❑ Completed application (if you completed the Common Application, include any requested supplemental forms).
- ❑ Completed financial-aid application.
- ❑ Application fee (or fee waiver).
- ❑ Slides of your work, if you are an artist or photographer.
- ❑ CD or DVD, if you are an athlete, musician, dancer, or in theater.
- ❑ Résumé or listing of your activities.

- [ ] Student essay (if one is required).
- [ ] Teacher recommendations (or recommendation requests if required).
- [ ] Stamped, self-addressed postcard listing all enclosed materials for admissions to check off and return to you or provide an e-mail address for confirmation.
- [ ] Transcript request form (and appropriate fee).
- [ ] With the exception of the transcript request form and fee, enclose all your information in a large envelope with the correct postage (at least two first class stamps).
- [ ] Attach the transcript request and fee to the outside of the envelope.
- [ ] Take your information to your counselor.

Be aware of your deadlines and turn this package in to your counselor at least 3 weeks before it is due.

# 69: send thank you notes

Thank you notes should be sent to:

- admissions officers or local interviewers if you are interviewed as part of the admissions process.

- your counselor, teachers, and others who give of their time to write recommendation letters.

- your counselor, coach, teachers, or others who assist you in applying to college, preparing for interviews, or packaging your scholarship applications.

- each organization where you apply for a scholarship, for considering your application whether or not you actually receive the scholarship.

- each person who presents you with a graduation gift or provides you with information that assists you in getting a scholarship or accepted into college.

# Chapter 14

## *Senior Year*

Your senior year will contain many important dates and deadlines. Get organized and get a calendar. To avoid missing out on college admissions and financial aid opportunities, you must know where your information is, you must mark important dates and deadlines on your calendar, and you must stay focused. By the beginning of your senior year, you should have completed your research, visited colleges, and identified the scholarships you will be applying for. You should already have arranged your list of schools into numerical order. The only thing that should cause you to change your mind at this point is a financial-aid award package from a school that was not on your list—an award amount that is so good that you must give the school and the financial-aid package serious consideration.

# 70: don't quit

**What if you are not accepted into your first-choice school?**

The reality is, thousands of students will receive letters from their first-choice schools denying them admission. Our younger son was denied admission to Brown, Penn, USC, and Northwestern. Thank God! We could not imagine any school that would have been better for him than Morehouse College. He is in the Honors College, he is a Gates Millennium Scholar, he has a great NROTC unit, and he is being both challenged and supported academically. He is attending a college that is vested in his success.

If you are denied admission to one or more of your first-choice colleges, do not allow it to discourage you from pursuing your dreams. If you are committed to your first-choice school then become proactive and continue planning to be admitted through the school's transfer program.

1. Write a letter to the admissions officer to reiterate that the school is your first choice.

2. Ask the admissions officer about the school's transfer policy.

3. Accept admissions to one of the schools that you have been admitted to which has the type of school community, major, and classes comparable to your first-choice school.

4. Schedule your classes based on the transfer course requirements at your first-choice school.

5. Enter college and make a positive contribution to the school that you enter while you continue to prepare yourself to be admitted as a transfer-student to your first-choice school.

However, like our son, you may find yourself among those students who are not admitted into their first-choice college, but who discover themselves treasuring the experience at the college where they ultimately enroll.

# References

The content of the book has been adapted from the book, *A High School Plan for Students with College-Bound Dreams*. Please refer to the larger text for complete references. Refer to *A High School Plan for Students with College-Bound Dreams: Workbook*, for a comprehensive set of activities and worksheets to assist students with developing their high school plan and tracking their progress.

Wynn, Mychal. (2005). *A High School Plan for Students with College-Bound Dreams*. Marietta, GA: Rising Sun Publishing.

Wynn, Mychal. (2006). *A High School Plan for Students with College-Bound Dreams: Workbook*. Marietta, GA: Rising Sun Publishing.

---

*Visit the Foundation for Ensuring Access and Equity's website. The college planning blog has links to scholarships, internships, summer programs, and a wide range of college planning resources. Although I love art, college has taught me how to be a great writer so I plan to do both.*

**www.accessandequity.org**

Mychal-David Wynn
Amherst College

---

# Index

# Texas Supplement

The Texas university system has 104 public institutions (38 universities, 50 community college districts, 9 health-related institutions, and 3 state colleges) and 44 independent institutions (39 universities, 2 junior colleges, 1 health-related institution, and 2 chiropractic institutions) providing students with a wide range of public and independent 2-year and 4-year colleges and universities offering a broad range of degree programs. Texas has 50 institutions identified as Hispanic Serving Institutions (HSIs) [*www.hacu.net*], defined by the U.S. Department of Education as having at least 25 percent Hispanic student enrollment. Texas has 9 institutions identified as Historically Black Colleges and Universities (HBCUs) defined by the U.S. Department of Education as a college or university established prior to 1964 with the principal mission of educating black Americans.

Each student must carefully consider whether to attend college close to home or across the state, with a few hundred students or with several thousand students, in a largely populated urban area or in a sparsely populated rural area, at a college with over a hundred years of history and tradition or at a college that is relatively new. Other factors for a student's consideration may be the religious focus of the college, whether a college is coed or single-gender, or whether the college is a major university or a liberal arts college? Will the cost of tuition, room, and board, together with the type of financial assistance offered by the college be an important consideration? Review the listing of Texas colleges and universities on the following pages and visit their websites.

The following websites will also assist with your college research:

- U.S. Department of Education Higher Education Center: *www.thecb.state.tx.us*

- Texas Higher Education Coordinating Board: *www.txhighereddata.org*

- College Results Online: *www.collegeresults.org/*

**Abilene Christian University**
*www.acu.edu*
**Alamo Community College District (HSI)**
*www.alamo.edu/nlc*
**Alamo Community College - St. Philip's College (HBCU/HSI)**
*www.alamo.edu/spc/*
**Alvin Community College**
*www.alvincollege.edu*
**Amarillo College**
*www.actx.edu*
**Amberton University**
*www.amberton.edu*
**Angelina College**
*www.angelina.edu*
**Angelo State University**
*www.angelo.edu*
**Austin College**
*www.austincollege.edu*
**Austin Community College District (HSI)**
*www.austincc.edu*
**Baylor College of Medicine**
*www.bcm.tmc.edu*
**Baylor University**
*www.baylor.edu*
**Blinn College**
*www.blinn.edu*

**Brazosport College**
*www.brazosport.edu*
**Brookhaven College (HSI)**
*www.brookhavencollege.edu*
**Cedar Valley College (HSI)**
*www.dcccd.edu/cvc/cvc.htm*
**Central Texas College**
*www.ctcd.edu*
**Cisco College**
*www.cisco.edu*
**Clarendon College**
*www.clarendoncollege.edu*
**Coastal Bend College (HSI)**
*vct.coastalbend.edu*
**College of Saints John Fisher & Thomas More**
*www.cstm.edu*
**College of the Mainland Community College District**
*www.com.edu*
**Collin County Community College District**
*www.collin.edu*
**Concordia University Texas**
*www.concordia.edu*
**Dallas Baptist University**
*www.dbu.edu*
**Dallas Community College District (HSI)**
*www.dcccd.edu/Pages/default.aspx*

**Del Mar College**
*www.delmar.edu*
**East Texas Baptist University**
*www.etbu.edu/default.htm*
**Eastfield College (HSI)**
*www.eastfieldcollege.edu*
**El Centro College (HSI)**
*www.ecc.dcccd.edu*
**El Paso Community College District (HSI)**
*www.epcc.edu*
**Frank Phillips College**
*www.fpctx.edu*
**Galveston College (HSI)**
*www.gc.edu*
**Grayson College**
*www.grayson.edu*
**Hardin-Simmons University**
*www.hsutx.edu*
**Hill College**
*www.hillcollege.edu/*
**Houston Baptist University**
*www.hbu.edu*
**Houston Community College System (HSI)**
*www.hccs.edu*
**Howard College**
*www.howardcollege.edu*

**Howard Payne University**
*www.hputx.edu*
**Huston - Tillotson University (HBCU)**
*www.htu.edu*
**Jacksonville College**
*www.jacksonville-college.edu*
**Jarvis Christian College (HBCU)**
*www.jarvis.edu*
**Kilgore College**
*www.kilgore.edu*
**Lamar Institute of Technology**
*www.lit.edu*
**Lamar State College - Orange**
*www.lsco.edu*
**Lamar State College - Port Arthur**
*www.lamarpa.edu*
**Lamar University**
*www.lamar.edu*
**Laredo Community College (HSI)**
*www.laredo.edu*
**Lee College (HSI)**
*www.lee.edu*
**LeTourneau University**
*www.letu.edu*
**Lon Morris College**
*www.lonmorris.edu*

**Lone Star College System (HSI)**
*www.lonestar.edu/*
**Lubbock Christian University**
*www.lcu.edu*
**McLennan Community College**
*www.mclennan.edu*
**McMurry University**
*www.mcm.edu/index.htm*
**Midland College (HSI)**
*www.midland.edu*
**Midwestern State University**
*www.mwsu.edu*
**Mountain View College (HSI)**
*www.mvc.dcccd.edu*
**Navarro College**
*www.navarrocollege.edu*
**North Central Texas College**
*www.nctc.edu*
**North Lake College (HSI)**
*www.northlakecollege.edu*
**Northeast Texas Community College**
*www.ntcc.edu*
**Odessa College**
*www.odessa.edu*
**Our Lady of the Lake University of San Antonio (HSI)**
*www.ollusa.edu*

**Panola College**
*www.panola.edu*
**Paris Junior College**
*www.parisjc.edu*
**Parker University**
*www.parker.edu*
**Paul Quinn College (HBCU)**
*www.pqc.edu*
**Prairie View A&M University (HBCU)**
*www.pvamu.edu*
**Ranger College**
*www.ranger.cc.tx.us*
**Rice University**
*www.rice.edu*
**Richland College (HSI)**
*www.rlc.dcccd.edu*
**Sam Houston State University**
*www.shsu.edu*
**San Jacinto College District (HSI)**
*www.sanjac.edu/*
**Schreiner University (HSI)**
*www.schreiner.edu*
**South Plains College**
*www.southplainscollege.edu*

**South Texas College (HSI)**
*www.southtexascollege.edu*
**South Texas College of Law**
*www.stcl.edu*
**Southern Methodist University**
*www.smu.edu*
**Southwest Collegiate Institute for the Deaf**
*www.howardcollege.edu/swcid/*
**Southwest Texas Junior College (HSI)**
*www.swtjc.net*
**Southwestern Adventist University (HSI)**
*www.swau.edu*
**Southwestern Assemblies of God University**
*www.sagu.edu*
**Southwestern Christian College (HBCU)**
*www.swcc.edu*
**Southwestern University**
*www.southwestern.edu*
**St. Edward's University (HSI)**
*www.stedwards.edu/*
**St. Mary's University (HSI)**
*www.stmarytx.edu*
**St. Phillip's College (HBCU)**
*www.alamo.edu/spc/*

**Stephen F. Austin State University**
*www.sfasu.edu*
**Sul Ross State University (HSI)**
*www.sulross.edu*
**Sul Ross State University Rio Grande College**
*www.sulross.edu*
**Tarleton State University**
*www.tarleton.edu*
**Tarrant County College**
*www.tccd.edu/*
**Tarrant County College District Trinity River Campus (HSI)**
*www.tccd.edu/Campuses_and_Centers/Trinity_River_Campus.html*
**Temple College**
*www.templejc.edu*
**Texarkana College**
*www.texarkanacollege.edu*
**Texas A&M International University (HSI)**
*www.tamiu.edu*
**Texas A&M University**
*www.tamu.edu*
**Texas A&M University at Galveston**
*www.tamug.edu*
**Texas A&M University System Health Science Center**
*tamhsc.edu*

**Texas A&M University - Central Texas**
*www.tarleton.edu/CENTRALTEXAS/*
**Texas A&M University - Commerce**
*www.tamuc.edu*
**Texas A&M University - Corpus Christi (HSI)**
*www.tamucc.edu*
**Texas A&M University - Kingsville (HSI)**
*www.tamuk.edu*
**Texas A&M University - San Antonio (HSI)**
*www.tamuk.edu/sanantonio/*
**Texas A&M University - Texarkana**
*www.tamut.edu*
**Texas Chiropractic College**
*www.txchiro.edu/*
**Texas Christian University**
*www.tcu.edu*
**Texas College (HBCU)**
*www.texascollege.edu*
**Texas Lutheran University (HSI)**
*www.tlu.edu*
**Texas Southern University (HBCU)**
*www.tsu.edu*
**Texas Southmost College (HSI)**
*www.utb.edu*

**Texas State Technical College Central Office**
*www.tstc.edu*
**Texas State Technical College - Harlingen (HSI)**
*www.harlingen.tstc.edu*
**Texas State Technical College - Marshall**
*www.marshall.tstc.edu*
**Texas State Technical College - Waco**
*www.waco.tstc.edu*
**Texas State Technical College - West Texas**
*www.westtexas.tstc.edu*
**Texas State University - San Marcos (HSI)**
*www.txstate.edu*
**Texas Tech University**
*www.ttu.edu*
**Texas Tech University Health Sciences Center**
*www.ttuhsc.edu*
**Texas Wesleyan University**
*www.txwes.edu*
**Texas Woman's University**
*www.twu.edu*
**Trinity University**
*www.trinity.edu*
**Trinity Valley Community College**
*www.tvcc.edu*

**Tyler Junior College**
*www.tjc.edu*
**University of Dallas**
*www.udallas.edu*
**University of Houston**
*www.uh.edu*
**University of Houston - Clear Lake (HSI)**
*www.uhcl.edu*
**University of Houston - Downtown (HSI)**
*www.uhd.edu*
**University of Houston - Victoria (HSI)**
*www.uhv.edu*
**University of Mary Hardin-Baylor**
*www.umhb.edu*
**University of North Texas**
*www.unt.edu*
**University of North Texas at Dallas (HSI)**
*www.unt.edu/unt-dallas/*
**University of North Texas Health Science Center**
*www.hsc.unt.edu*
**University of St. Thomas**
*www.stthom.edu*
**University of Texas at Arlington**
*www.uta.edu*

**University of Texas at Austin**
*www.utexas.edu*
**University of Texas at Brownsville (HSI)**
*www.utb.edu*
**University of Texas at Dallas**
*www.utdallas.edu*
**University of Texas at El Paso (HSI)**
*www.utep.edu*
**University of Texas at San Antonio (HSI)**
*www.utsa.edu*
**University of Texas at Tyler**
*www.uttyler.edu*
**University of Texas Health Science Center at Houston**
*www.uth.tmc.edu*
**University of Texas Health Science Center at San Antonio (HSI)**
*www.uthscsa.edu*
**University of Texas Health Science Center at Tyler**
*www.uthct.edu*
**University of Texas M.D. Anderson Cancer Center**
*www.mdanderson.org/healthsciences*
**University of Texas Medical Branch at Galveston**
*www.utmb.edu*
**University of Texas of the Permian Basin (HSI)**
*www.utpb.edu*

**University of Texas - Pan American (HSI)**
*www.panam.edu*
**University of Texas Southwestern Medical Center**
*www.utsouthwestern.edu/student*
**University of the Incarnate Word (HSI)**
*www.uiw.edu*
**Vernon College**
*www.vernoncollege.edu*
**Victoria College (HSI)**
*www.victoriacollege.edu*
**Wayland Baptist University**
*www.wbu.edu*
**Weatherford College**
*www.wc.edu*
**West Texas A&M University**
*www.wtamu.edu*
**Western Texas College (HSI)**
*www.wtc.edu*
**Wharton County Junior College**
*www.wcjc.edu*
**Wiley College (HBCU)**
*www.wileyc.edu*

*Visit the following website for the complete listing of Texas Colleges and Universities:*
*www.window.state.tx.us/scholars/schools/*

*College Planning Quick Guide: Texas Edition*
*ISBN 978-1880463-58-1*
*Price: $5.95*

*To order additional copies, learn about sponsorship opportunities, personalize copies for your school or school district, or to purchase large quantities, contact:*

*Rising Sun Publishing*
*P.O. Box 70906*
*Marietta, GA 30007*
*Phone: (770) 518-0369*
*FAX: (770) 587-0862*
*E-mail: info@rspublishing.com*
*Order online: www.rspublishing.com*